Confessions of a Bank Financier

Sharing Secrets Your Bank Doesn't Want You To Know... That Will Save You Thousands!

By

Sua Van Truong

Keep on dreaming

To your Success!

1st Edition – February 2015

Library and Archives Canada Cataloguing in Publications

Truong, Sua, Van 1970 –
    Confessions of a Bank Financier

ISBN: 0993930905
ISBN-13: 978-0-993930904

Dedication

This book is dedicated to my father who taught me the meaning of
hard work and the importance of having full integrity.
I am grateful for the eternal support of my loving family during my
journey. Thank you my sweetheart, Tuyet Mai Lu and my
wonderful daughters Kyla and Luna.
You guys are the reason why I do what I do!

Acknowledgements

Many thanks to my mentors Colin Sprake, Iman Aghay and
Camilo Rodriguez for helping me on my journey.
Thank you to my great friends and amazing clients that have been
a part of my journey.
Special thanks to my editors Diane Chesson and Wayne Purdin.

FOREWORD

Sua has finally put his 15 years of experience in the financial services industry into a book. All you ever need to know about financial services industry is diluted in this book!

It is refreshing to read this candid book by maverick mortgage broker, Sua Van Truong. He openly tells customers what to look for and what to avoid. Not just with mortgages but with credit and insurance products. Whether you're someone who wants to save money in real estate or someone in the finance industry who wants to increase your clientele, this book will help you accomplish those goals.

Sua is no stranger to fraud, having been a victim himself along with thousands of other investors perpetrated by Eron Mortgage Corporation in the late1990's. This motivated him to acquire all the financial knowledge that he could through various roles in the financial industry.

Sua wanted to have the biggest impact on helping families. He decided to become an independent mortgage broker because a property is the largest investment asset and debt that anyone can have. He is one of a few mortgage brokers that truly treat his clients as if they were his own family. Sua is compassionate and passionate about his mission to help people avoid the mistakes he made. Warning the public about the credit, insurance, and mortgage traps he acknowledges are still out there in the financial jungle.

In *Confessions of a Bank Financier,* Sua openly shares industry information that bankers and insurance agents are reluctant to let the public know, some of which can potentially save customers thousands of dollars.

Sua has been involved in the financial services industry for over 15 years. During that time, he learned what does and doesn't work, what to say, when to say and how to say it. In the process, he discovered a formula that has helped him grow his mortgage broker business from being an average income earner to tripling his income in less than 18 months. Whether you are an advisor or sales person, you can use the formula revealed in this book to achieve massive success in your business. In fact, some of Sua's 14 secrets of success are good tips for success in any profession.

This book has the potential of changing the face of the finance industry. The general public will read it, become savvier when shopping for a mortgage or insurance, and won't be fooled so easily. They will be able to "turn the table on the cold corporate banking world," as Sua puts it. Mortgage brokers will read it and follow the principles that led to Sua's success without taking advantage of their clients. They can recognize the weakness in the finance industry and join him in working on changing it.

Confessions of a Bank Financier is not just an intellectual read, but a balanced one with love, wisdom, and power. The love is felt in the very personal tone of his writing, in which he opens his heart to the reader with stories from his life, and in his honesty about his motivation. The wisdom is evident in the philosophy he shares, born from a lifetime of entrepreneurship and ethical conduct. Sua promises, "The more you know, the less they will profit from your ignorance."

Raymond Aaron, Best-selling author, the nation's number #1 success and investment coach.

Table of Contents

Introduction

Why Did I Write This Book?

In my 15+ years working in the financial services industry, you could say I've seen and heard it all. I wish that were true. I learn new things every day, and it never ceases to amaze me how many bad things happen to good people inside the industry. I want to share with you what I have seen and experienced in those years.

By arming you with this knowledge, you will be able to turn the table on the cold corporate banking world. You will be able to legally take advantage of opportunities that the banks would not have wanted you to. Why should corporations reap huge wealth beyond your dreams when the average family is just barely able to get by? I felt that there were just too many injustices being piled onto the consumer, and no one was helping the little guys out. I was one of those little guys.

At 25 years of age, I lost all the money I had made, my trusted friends' life savings and my father's life savings. I thought I knew enough to invest in real estate. I did my research but inevitably trusted the mortgage broker I was working with. He was also the Vice President of the company (the infamous Eron Mortgage Corporation). I knew the value of money and knew how hard it was to earn since I had run several businesses from the age of 15. I had learned quickly about money, debt and the compound interest monster, but none of those prepared me for my first big failure. Eron Mortgage Corporation and its directors swindled more than $200 million dollars from Canadians. We were part of the casualties.

The money was eventually regained, but the loss of trust was more devastating and affected me for much longer. I remember at that time I had asked myself, "Who would do something as evil as this? Why be so greedy and hurt so many people that have depended on their savings to help them in their retirement?" I thought to myself, "How could anyone do this?" Isn't there a mortgage broker that won't lie, cheat and take advantage of people? Is there no one out there that has the integrity to help people with their finances anymore? I thought, "Why not me?" This event was the impetus that propelled me to change my career and eventually become a mortgage broker. I felt that there has to be someone who can offer trustworthy service and impartial advice that anyone can rely on to protect him from making the same mistakes that I had made. I wrote this book so that other people would not have to go through similar experiences and the pain that I had.

Intentions - my intention for writing this book is to inform the public of things that happen behind the scenes and the underlying reasons. It is only to inform people and not to shame the people in this industry although shaming them probably wouldn't change anything. People inside the industry could look at it in two different ways: One, they could react negatively to what I have written as if I had opened up a Pandora's box, or two, they could take what I wrote and use it in a positive way. They could recognize the weakness I have pinpointed and work on changing part of the process or strategy. I believe there's always a place for any business to thrive as long as the intention is to put the client's best interest first at all times.

I also wanted to point out that the majority of people out there have a flaw in their financial plans. Most people have financial advisors helping them take care of their assets, but most of them have very few assets. A home is the largest debt and should require the most attention, yet people don't have anyone helping them manage that debt. Which makes more sense? Just leaving it to the bank or having an unbiased advisor help manage it for them? What makes more sense for you?

Who Is This Book For?

This book is for you if you are:
- Worried about your money and overwhelmed with too many online experts' advice.
- Worried if your financial institutions are taking advantage of you.
- Confused about how credit or debt really works.
- Interested in getting a piece of the bank's billion dollar record profit.
- Interested in helping people with their finances or investments.
- Looking for someone who is not afraid to tell it like it is.

If any of those applies to you, then this book was meant for you.

This book is dedicated to those tireless souls that are in a position of trust as advisors or dealing with people's money, doing their best to make a difference. Those who truly place their client's best interest first (before themselves); you are the reason why this book was written!

How To Make the Best Use of This Book:

It is broken down into separate sections and subsections. The first half of the book is for the general public and the last half is for industry professionals. However, the true benefit is for those that read the entire book. That way you benefit by having a better understanding of both sides of the industry. The more you understand the more power you have. You will be able to relate to every party at the table much better. I've heard this saying many times: "The less I know, the more they make." I hope what I pass on in this book will change that to, "The more I know, the less they profit from my ignorance."

My Story

The Early Years

I was born into a family of successful entrepreneurs but in a country that was quickly imploding upon itself. At that time I was a young child in South Vietnam. The Americans had lost the war and left our country to fend for itself. Our country was being taken over by the Communists.

Our family fled with what little we had and headed for Thailand. During the journey, we encountered pirates and lost whatever remaining possessions we had to those pirates at sea. By the time we arrived in Thailand, we were poorer than beggars on the street. We remained refugees for nearly a year and eventually got sponsored to Canada by a kind Christian family.

It took us a while, but our family eventually duplicated the success we had in Vietnam. My father only worked for one employer in his whole life, and that was when we first came to Canada. He was a jack of all trade and tried anything that could earn him money or make him seem like an expert in that field.

I learned a lot while growing up in our entrepreneurial family. I also learned that working harder and longer hours would cut your lifespan shorter, as it did to my father at the age of 52.

I vowed that this would not be my path.

My Transformation

After several years of working in the financial services field and building my own family, I allowed that promise I made to myself fade away into oblivion until one day when I was abruptly awakened from my slumber.

My 16 plus hours-a-day work-life was finally taking a toll on our family. I was nearing the end of my second year as an independent mortgage broker and finally seeing some real success. My wife approached me one night when I arrived home late and asked, "When are you going to be home to say goodnight to your kids?" It floored me. I did not realize I was doing the exact same thing that I had vowed not to do. I had watched my father work 16 plus hours a day growing up.

Her question had the same effect as if waking a person from a lucid dream. I suddenly realized I was coming close to doing exactly what my father had done. I knew right then and there that I had to make a change. Working harder was doubling my income, but at what cost?

I couldn't go to my peers for help since many of them have achieved similar success in the industry by doing exactly the same thing -- working harder, which really equated to working longer hours. I had to find a different way. In the following years, I invested heavily in myself by enlisting mentors and hiring business coaches to help me work smarter. I will share with you what I learned in the process and how I doubled and tripled my income.

The Credit Monster

School of Hard Knocks

Like many students, I graduated from college with a large debt I had amassed over the years. Yes, I heard about students graduating with crushing debt and ending up in mediocre paying jobs, but I thought that I would do better than that. Was I ever wrong! That was the first test of my eternal optimism.

I don't blame anybody but myself. It all started on that fateful day when I was handed a bag full of goodies from the university's welcoming committee. Inside that bag were 2 pre-approved credit card applications for students. At that time I never gave it much thought and as a joke, I applied for both. Guess what? I received the two credit cards shortly after. Like most students, I spent more than I should have. That easy access to credit was the beginning of my debt and my compound interest lesson.

Why anyone would give unemployed students credit cards the minute they enter college is really beyond me. Looking back this seems like a bad joke being told by a really bad comedian. This is not a great way to teach responsibility to students. The majority of full time students are not employed and on those applications, the credit card companies were okay with "student" as the status of employment. This is how it all starts. When you are a full time student, getting in debt is very easy. Since most don't have enough time to make much money, it becomes very hard to get out of the vicious debt cycle.

Cashing in Your Chips and Taking a Permanent Vacation

I heard this funny quote once, "Your credit is so bad that your mother wouldn't lend you money." At that time I thought it was hilarious. I didn't realize that many years later, I wouldn't be laughing at that joke in the same way again.

The thing about credit is that it can be a double edged sword. Having too much credit tells potential new lenders that you are a notorious credit seeker, and they may not be that willing to lend anymore. I once met a client that had more than 30 credit cards. I didn't even think that was possible. I asked him why. He said it's like collecting hockey cards. He shows them off to his friends. In my mind I shook my head. That was not a good reason at all. Now if he had said, "One day I'll cash my chips in and take a permanent vacation…" Okay, so not another good reason either but at least that would have been much funnier to hear and at least makes some sense. On the other hand, having no credit is not good either since the majority of things that you do requires credit worthiness everywhere you go. Building credit is a must. However, no one is given the "How to Build Your Credit Properly" instruction manual with his credit cards. There are a lot of misconceptions out there, and in this chapter you will learn enough to help you win this credit game.

Giving Credit Where Credit Is Due

Here are some common myths and general misconceptions about credit (credit scores) that you should understand. The following 9 tips will give you a blueprint to improve your credit:

- Applying for credit at many places at once would hurt my credit score. True and false. Shopping for some types of credit does affect your score, but auto loans and mortgages are usually lumped together and depending on the time frame, may not impact the score at all. All inquiries made within 14 days when shopping for a car loan/lease or mortgages are counted as only one inquiry. However, shopping for credit cards or consumer loans will reduce the beacon score.

- It will build my credit if I pay off the balance on my card each month. True and false. Yes it will, but having a small balance that you pay the minimum balance each month actually does the same. In some cases, it's better to have a small balance and pay the minimum to build your credit if your credit is new. They are more likely to increase your limit in the future. This in turn may help your score.

- If I use up my entire credit limit on my card (ie. to get loyalty points), and pay it off, my credit will be better. False. Depending on when your credit status is updated from the credit card issuer, it may show that you max out your credit card all the time to the potential lenders. This is not a good thing. Anyone using up more than 75% of the limit may actually be hurting their credit score.

- If I am over my limit (some credit card company allows you to go over X amount like 10%) and pay it off, it won't affect my credit. False. Same as above scenario. Double whammy since this is one of the most punishing thing (other than collections/bankruptcy) that you can do to your credit score. The minute you go one cent above your credit limit, your score is negatively affected.

- If I am late a few days and pay it up completely, my credit should be okay. False. This is not the same banking world that my grandfather and great grandfather were used to. In those days, that was acceptable. If you are even one day late, that will lower your score.

- I'll skip paying the minimum this month and make it up next month. This inaction will damage your credit. Paying a lot one month and not paying the minimum the next month does the same damage to your credit file.

- If I pay early on the weekend and it's due on Monday, it is paying on time, right? False! It depends on how you made your payment. If you paid it online on Friday evening, your payment will not be processed for at least two to three business days and the creditor will deem your payment as late. If you are going to pay on the due date, pay it in person.

- If I have one credit card with a huge limit (say $20,000+), that's all I need to build credit right? False. Many lenders would prefer someone with two or three different sources of credit established with a $2000 credit limit each rather than just one source with a huge credit limit.

- I have a really old $500 credit card I never use, there's no harm in cancelling it right? False. Matter of fact, that very old card actually has a much higher "credit value" on the beacon score than a large credit card you recently acquired. It's the same thing as having a really old but poor friend compared to having a really wealthy new friend. Who do you trust more? Does that make sense?

CAVEAT EMPTOR (Latin for "buyers beware")

Have you ever bought something and found out afterwards that what you bought was not what you paid for? If anyone has paid for a credit report by purchasing it online, he or she would have found out that that report is not the same as what the bank or other lenders get. As a matter of fact, the credit score never matches and is normally an inflated number compared to what the bank would see. I won't go into a long story with this but the results that you receive are different because the valuation algorithms are different.

The free report that you can get by filling in a form and mailing it to them does not give you a precise "beacon score" but a range. The free credit report that you receive is actually more useful but will take time to request and have it sent to you by regular mail. My word of advice is to save that money and do it the slow way. No point in paying for disappointment. "Caveat Emptor" applies.

You can go to my website (www.SharingBankSecrets.com) for a detailed explanation of how the different credit bureaus grade your credit score and how you can increase your score.

You can request for your free credit report from the following credit bureau by going to their website:

www.Equifax.ca
or
www.TransUnion.ca

The Rule of 72 (a.k.a. Compound Interest Monster)

Einstein once said, "Compound interest is the eighth wonder of the world. He who understands it, earns it ... he who doesn't ... pays it."

It is pretty sad that the financial institutions are willing to entrap young adults into the vicious debt cycle but do very little to educate them. I guess teaching them how money works (such as compound interest a.k.a. the "Rule of 72") would not be very profitable for them. Of course not!

The RULE of 72 in ACTION

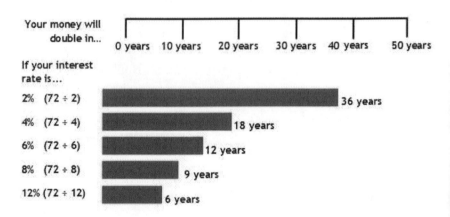

Your money will double in...	0 years	10 years	20 years	30 years	40 years	50 years

If your interest rate is...

2% (72 ÷ 2)	36 years
4% (72 ÷ 4)	18 years
6% (72 ÷ 6)	12 years
8% (72 ÷ 8)	9 years
12% (72 ÷ 12)	6 years

The rule of 72 is a simple explanation of how compound interest works to the lay person. Basically, if you divide the interest rate into 72, the answer that you get is the number of years it would take for the money to double. For example, if you have 12% interest and an amount of $10,000 it would take 6 years for that amount to grow to $20,000. In 48 years, it would be a whopping $2.5M!

This is great if you were investing, but it can be a hideous, scary monster if the amount is debt that you owe. If I had known about the rule of 72 and looked at the interest on my credit card, I would have realized that the money I borrowed would have doubled by the time I graduated ($72 \div 19.9\% = 3.6$ years). By paying the minimum payments, it would have taken me several years more to pay it off! More shockingly, I would have paid several times what I had spent.

Saying yes, I should have listened to my parents and only bought what I could afford to pay in cash is really not the answer. Everything today is built on the credit system, and you have to have good credit to borrow money. You need really big amounts of money to make more money. The answer is not to use cash but to learn how to play the game and play it better.

The information I have compiled in this book will empower people and give them an advantage over the bank rather than being at their mercy all the time. The financial institutions have always had an unfair advantage over the consumer. I felt that after working for many years at the bank and only pushing what I was told to offer, even if I did not feel good about doing it, people should know the truth. It's time to push back.

Why am I doing this? Why do I ask these tough questions? When you genuinely care about people, you ask tough questions rather than skirt around the issue.

The Life Insurance Hoax

You're Worth More Dead than Alive?

For some people that phrase is not amusing; it's probably their reality. There are several forms of life insurance in the market. The three main types are "Whole Life", "Universal Life" and "Term" insurance. I won't go into full details about how each product works but just cover an overview of what each is and why you should want to buy each type or avoid it. Let me preface that I am not all against life insurance agents and that I am not 100% against permanent life insurance. What I am against is the fact that the majority of agents out there promote only the most expensive whole life insurance to everyone they come across. Most push it aggressively because of the high commissions they can earn compared to the term insurance product.

The main difference between "Term" insurance and the other two permanent life insurance products is that term is very simple to understand. Term insurance is like your home or auto insurance: if you die, they pay. If you don't, you're lucky. It has no bells or whistle. Whole life has a small insurance coverage and a savings component. Universal life is very similar with added complexity on the investment component (mutual funds or segregated funds). Trying to decipher how the investment portion works or how much of your monthly payment gets invested requires a PHD degree. The majority of life insurance agents do not know exactly how it is calculated. It is aggravating to go through their complex process to figure it out. Save yourself the grief; keep it simple. Buy what you understand and know how much of your money is being invested each month.

If you buy the wrong type of life insurance policy, you could waste a ton of money and still leave your family inadequately protected. Despite this danger, some agents still try to mislead consumers into buying the wrong type. Sometimes they do this because they make a ton more in commissions when they sell you whole life or other types of permanent life insurance (like universal life) as opposed to term insurance. Other times, they try to sell this monstrosity because they actually believe their own misguided sales pitch. Most life insurance companies are excellent at brainwashing their agents into truly believing that it is good for their clients. If they had done their own research instead of listening to the organization's propaganda, they would know better.

True Pitch, False Pitch?

At the end of the day, their motivation does not really matter. What matters is that you don't fall into this permanent life trap if you are like the vast majority of people who don't need it. Here are the five main pitches some agents use on unsuspecting clients:

1. "Don't you love your family?"
Permanent life insurance agents can use guilt to get you to buy. They claim that if you have dependents and don't buy their insurance, you are irresponsible.

Well, if you have dependents you certainly might need life insurance. Even if you do, it doesn't mean you need their expensive and high commission-paying life insurance. You can buy a heck of a lot more term insurance (often 10 times more insurance) for the same premium you get with permanent coverage. Logically speaking, you might say that people who buy term life care ten times more about their family than people who buy whole or universal life.

2. "It's forced savings."
This is true, but it isn't the only means to do it. The sad reality is that the investment returns on the majority if not all permanent insurance have been abysmal compared to similar investment vehicles outside of a life insurance product. If you want a way to create forced savings, why not setup a monthly contribution towards a separate investment that automatically gets withdrawn from your bank account? You have more control over the investments and save a bundle on fees that otherwise would have been incurred inside an insurance product. Permanent life insurance has historically given lousy returns. The argument of forced savings is a bold-faced lie.

4. "You can borrow from it."
In a permanent life insurance policy, you have the savings component called "cash surrender value" that accumulates over time. Usually, there is nothing in that savings component during the first two to five years since they have been used up to pay the agent's commission. Certain whole life or universal life policies will allow you to withdraw your "forced savings" from the policy. However, you have to "borrow" your own savings and must repay that amount; otherwise, your policy will lapse. Yes, it boggles my mind every time I hear this pitch being used. If I invested my own money and withdraw from it, I don't have to pay it back if I don't want. Since my term insurance is purchased separately and not tied to my investment, it does not affect my life insurance whatsoever. Matter of fact, I can "borrow" my own savings without ever having to repay it. Borrowing from your own savings is a scam!

4. "It's always there."
Life insurance agents argue that permanent insurance is always there, unlike term insurance. That is not always the case. The majority of people cancel the coverage well before they make a claim. According to Consumer Reports, 40% of permanent life insurance buyers cancel their policies within the first 10 years. The primary reason for cancellation is that it is too expensive.

22

It is debatable that those people even need the insurance in the first place. According to independent financial advisors, life insurance is really most important between the ages of 25 to 40. When you are first starting a family, liabilities are huge and investments are near zero; insurance need is greatest at that phase of our life. As we get older and more savings have accumulated, the need decreases for most people. A small percentage of people may still need it but most likely much less. Chances are most people would not be affected as much since their savings could help cushion most life events.

5. "You may not be insurable in the later years."
This is the only argument that may be valid. However, it really only applies if you need to get life insurance for 100 years. The sad reality is that if you have a real financial advisor helping you take care of your investments properly, you should not need life insurance in your retirement. A little coverage may be needed for estate planning. Over the span of 20 years from 45 to 65, you should be able to save over $120,000 in savings if you purchased term insurance over permanent life insurance. A financial advisor should be able to turn that saving into a tidy nest egg. This argument would be considered a joke at that point. I mean seriously, at 65 the kids should all have grown up and left the home. The mortgage should have been paid off or nearly paid off. Living expense should be a lot less, and your government retirement supplement should have kicked in by then. Why do you still need life insurance?

The only real benefit is to the surviving adult children that may want a bigger windfall. If you had the common sense to purchase term insurance and then you invested the difference over the years, I am certain that you taught your children well enough so that they won't need handouts. The true beneficiary of spending five to ten times the cost of a permanent life insurance is to the life insurance agent. I would rather invest that money elsewhere and receive a comfortable 55 to 8% return on my money. With compound interest, that would amount to over three hundred thousand dollars without adding more money than the difference in cost of the life insurance. I would pocket all that money when I retire and leave whatever is left to my children after I am gone.

My father passed away just as most of the kids in the family hit adulthood. It didn't affect any of us financially, and our family was able to continue on as usual. If he had passed away when we were kids, it would have been devastating. So, I don't buy that you need life insurance for your whole life. If my father had purchase the permanent insurance, he would have scraped every month to pay for it since it would have been too costly for the same coverage. I believe none of the kids would be happy seeing our father sacrifice his standard of living to pay for a life insurance product like that.

Why would I want to contribute to a life insurance agent's pay check? I am sure some life insurance agents reading this are fuming right now.

For those that fall for the "paid up" life insurance guarantee, I have news for you. They misled you. What the agent sold you was not what they actually gave you. They did warn you inside that policy that you signed for that the life insurance amount and duration were not truly guaranteed. My colleague had a client that paid into a universal life policy for over 25 years and thought it was paid up. Now in his retirement, he has to continue paying for it to keep the same coverage or have it dramatically reduced if he wants the insurance to pay for itself. Yes, he would also lose every penny in the savings component as well.

Paid up life insurance is also a bold faced lie. Nothing in life is free, especially when it comes to life insurance.

The Banker's Bag of Secrets

Have you ever wondered why even in a downturn in the economy, banks always make a record profit? Billions and billions! -- even in the lowest interest rate climate that we have. Have you wondered why? Look at mortgage rates. They are at a historic all time low and have dropped below 3% at the time of writing this book. The question is, why are mortgages still so profitable for the banks? Hint: It's not the interest that they earn. The answers can be found below.

Have you ever gone into a bank and seen those charts listing interest rates for products and loans? Mortgages for example have two sets of rates. The discounted rates and the posted rates are posted side by side. Why do you think they do that? Most people have no idea. It's a safe bet to think that banks don't just do something like posting numbers on their wall for no reason. Would it make sense that there must be a reason why those high numbers called "Posted Rates" are shown in the bank and on their websites? Of course, but what could it be for? Have you ever wondered that? A majority of the public has no idea and never even considered asking about the relevance of those "posted rates." If they had, they would be shocked to find out the true reason for them.

Let's look at how the banks make money. Well at least how the consumer thinks the banks make money. One of their biggest products is mortgage financing on property. It takes hundreds of thousands of dollars to finance a home. The public is lead to believe that this is where they make the most money from. In a way they do but not from the source that you would expect.

Now, let's look at the mortgage product itself. If your business had a $300,000 product and only made $2,000 profit per sale, how could you survive? How could you make record profits year in and year out? Due to the cost of money, the profit that the banks make on mortgages is so small. If a business owner's profit margin is what the bank enjoys on their mortgage products, they would be out of business in a short time. How can a bank make so much money even when the economy is doing so badly? How can they thrive when most businesses are barely able to survive?

How about looking at this from a different perspective? What if I sold you a lease on a car that comes with a 5 year term of ownership and a significant penalty will be incurred if you change the term of the contract within the 5 years (ie. selling the car or returning it early). Matter of fact, the penalty would be much higher than the total interest paid over the 5 years. Would you take the lease on that car? Of course you wouldn't. Well I have news for you. Many people have unwittingly done just that with their home. All fixed mortgages from retail lenders work this way. Wholesale lenders are different. I will discuss that later.

The dirty secret is that they make most of their money on the back end of the mortgage. Mortgage penalties are a huge cash cow for the banks. Even though the bank loses interest earned on your mortgage when you cancel the mortgage before the maturity, they don't calculate that amount fairly. They use one set of rates for your mortgage interest payments but a different set of rates for the penalty. How fair is that?

When the bank needs to increase their profit, guess what they do? All they need to do is just raise their posted rate. It won't have any effect on people coming in to get financing since nobody ever signs up for the posted rate on their mortgage. They won't even notice a thing. In fact, it would mostly be ignored since the public considers posted rate as irrelevant to them. Sadly, though, it's quite the opposite and consumers are misled into believing that it doesn't apply to them. This has cost many people so much of their hard-earned money. They say ignorance is bliss. In this case, being ignorant will cost you every penny you had invested.

Over the years, I've heard so many clients tell me that their bank advisors had only told them they would be penalized with three months' worth of interest penalties. Sadly, most advisors at the bank level do not have the time to spend with the clients to go into details as to how the penalties are calculated or how much would be incurred. Bank employees have to juggle many roles and have to cover numerous products that they need to sell. The advisors usually generalize the mortgage penalty part and most often mistakenly refer to what borrowers would pay in penalties as if it were a floating term instead of a fixed term. Sometimes it is due to lack of education on the bank employee's part, but most of the time it is due to time constraints that are placed on them. Sad to say, but they need to get you out before the next appointment.

You Get What You Pay for...You Thought...

If you want to spend sufficient time for real education about the process and complexity of mortgage products in the market, talk to a mortgage broker. They will spend hours on the subject that they have invested 100% of their time on. They are the specialists, while banks which are generalists. Even better, talk to an independent mortgage broker and find a wholesale lender that only has one set of rates instead of two.

Most people don't believe that they will ever be in a situation that would make them incur a mortgage penalty. However, the industry statistic shows that over 40% of mortgage holders will incur some sort of life event that will trigger a mortgage penalty. When it does, guess who wins? The bank and their shareholders win. It's definitely not you or me.

Wholesale lenders are mostly accessible through a network of independent mortgage brokers. They usually do not have a sales force or front line staff to accept applications for loans. By not having a large staff of front line workers, they have very little overhead and can operate profitably using an existing network or brokers to drive them business. They simplify their process and product line. They only have one set of rates and use the same set of rates to calculate mortgage penalties.

Should You Ask the Enemy for Help?

Nobody wants lip service but we all accept it and take it at face value. Even though nobody wants to be a sheep, we all allow big corporations to treat us like sheep. The "ugly truth" is a reality that is distasteful or painful to accept, but because it is known to be true, one must accept it. In the banking world, it happens often but nobody is willing to talk about it or even wants to bring it up. Sort of like an elephant in the room. It's a big eyesore, but nobody is willing to admit it's a problem. The fact is, it's rarely a good thing for the bank or the professional representing the lender to bring it up. Think twice; think really hard before asking for help because you might not like the answer. Or lack of answer.

I'll give you an example. When I worked at the bank and knew that our competitor had a better product than us, I could not even tell my clients about it. Even if a client had asked me if this were the best that they could get, I could only tell them that this is the best that our bank can offer them currently. If I told them the other bank across the street has a better offer, I would have been fired. If we could not help them and I knew that a competitor could, I could not tell my potential client this information either. Why? You guess it. I would risk the chance of being fired from my job for trying to do what I felt was the right thing to do. This was an unwritten law that must be adhered to by every employee who didn't want to risk termination.

I had to be politically neutral when dealing with clients on their investments but not so when acquiring more debt. We were encouraged to sell as many bank products as possible so that it would be hard for any customer to leave us. Along this line, there was a very concerning trend that I saw. It was the grey area between cross selling and tied selling that more and more employees were skirting. With cross selling the advisor offers you other products or services to buy or sign up for so that it would increase the profit received from each customer. Tied selling is when you are being forced to buy a secondary product in order to receive the primary product or service. There is a grey area between these two that many bank employees are being indirectly pushed to cross. All bank employees are being coerced to do it even if they do not feel it is good for the client. "Why," you ask?

Many corporations are using periodic reviews on their employees to gauge performance. The banks are not making an exception. The fear of performing poorly on their "performance reviews" would make any good hearted soul cross that line and go beyond the grey area. If not, he better start hunting for a new job early.

Don't get me wrong, it's not the people in the industry who are bad. It is the system and the way it is set up that is not in line with our nature. As much as we want to help our fellow human beings 100% of the time, the corporate structure prevents us from doing so. Corporations are in the business of making money for their shareholders, not their customers or their employees. Employees and customers are part of the profit making model. Part of that profit model is driven by performance-based compensation or performance based reviews for employees.

Bank Mortgage Insurance

Making Money Out of Thin Air

Other than increasing deposits from customers, mortgage insurance is one product that has been pushed the most to increase profit. Why? Bank mortgage insurance is the most profitable product that a bank can sell. It is an intangible product that has a decreasing cost to the bank or insurer. What do I mean by that? Well, your debt will be lowered as the years go by and eventually you will owe less and less. If you tragically pass away in the later years, they only have to pay that lower amount of debt. So, the longer the customer has the insurance, the less the bank or insurer has to pay on a claim.

I have met many clients over the years that told me they felt that they had to buy the mortgage insurance to qualify for the lower rate on their mortgage. It sounds like a borderline tied selling scenario. Remember, tied selling is the act of forcing someone to buy something in order to get that other item or service. It is actually illegal in most countries (if not everywhere). Tied selling is against the law. When your performance review is coming and your job may be in jeopardy due to under-performing, you may just push a bit harder to get the client to buy it.

These circumstances and scenarios I detailed are not fiction. Matter of fact, it is a daily re-occurring event that happens in our industry. It should undeniably show you that there is a huge conflict of interest when you are dealing with the banks.

The House Always Wins - in Mortgage Insurance

Bank mortgage insurance is not a scam. It does come close though. It is mainly good for making money for the bank and their shareholders.

Here are a few other nasty reasons why you should not buy bank mortgage insurance:

- They cost much more than an equivalent term insurance from an independent life insurance company. Many times double the cost on a comparable term insurance from an outside insurance company (such as Manulife, London Life, TransAmerica etc).
- Unlike non-bank insurance, they are post-claim underwritten. This means that they will collect your premium but not guarantee to pay your claim until you can prove the death is legitimate and insurance was qualified. This means they will not pay if they can argue that death was a result of a pre-existing condition. If a medical record shows that death was caused by a previous health issue with high blood pressure or a past injury that aggravated the illness, you pay, but chances are they won't!
- Not portable. This means your insurance will terminate if you decide to move your mortgage to a different lender. Which may be a problem now that you are older (insurance cost increases) and if you are no longer insurable due to health issues. Non-bank insurance companies offer products that are portable and it does not matter who you got your mortgage from.
- Finally, the mortgage insurance only pays the bank off. Not you or your family. You're paying for the original amount of the insurance but they forget to tell you that over time the amount they pay will be only the amount you currently owe. No extra money to go to your family. So, really, whose interest are they really serving?

For these and many other reasons, I recommend that everyone avoid bank mortgage insurance. Find a reputable, independent life insurance agent to help with those needs instead. Contact me via email if you need a referral to a reputable one.

The Down-Payment Juggling Act

Guilty Money Launderer Until Proven Innocent!

I was told that in a democratic country like ours, you are innocent until proven guilty. For some reason I feel that the financial system we have does not embrace this rule. For instance, when you are in the process of purchasing a property, sometimes you beg and borrow to get the money required for the down payment. Most people pool it all together into one place to prepare for the purchase of their dream home or investment property.

So now that you have money for the down payment to purchase your dream home, let's get financing for the rest. Hold on there! Not so fast. If you had made large deposits into your bank account recently (past 30-90 days), your bank may not allow you to use it right away. You see, FINTRAC (Financial Transactions and Reports Analysis Centre of Canada) may suspect that you are laundering money. Other countries around the world have similar organizations that do the same. In the eyes of these regulators that oversee the bank, any deposits over $10,000 in a short period of time may put you under suspicion as a potential money launderer or as someone associated with a potential terrorist organization

You will have to wait at least 30 days or up to 90 days before you can use that fund unless you can prove unequivocally that the source of that money is legitimate. If that money was sent from out of the country, you may be required to wait regardless.

Hurdles like this have hurt many legitimate citizens over the years and in certain situations have made the purchase of a home even more costly. Some found a way to overcome this by financing it with private lenders and transferring the mortgage over to a bank lender at a later date. The government understands that a percentage of society does not trust the banks and keep their savings under their mattresses. I have met several "baby boomers" who have actually saved their money at home and given it to their kids to purchase their first property. The problem is that the parents do not have a documented account for the source of those funds. Declaring it as a gifted fund is one thing, but having a bank allow it is another. Is it fair to punish law abiding citizens?

Governments are pushing more people to declare their earnings and have put in place many hurdles like these to squeeze more tax dollars out of their citizens.

Playing by the Rules or With the Rules?

Occasionally, I have clients asking me whether or not they can purchase an investment property with 5% down. The official answer is NO. Unfortunately, only a primary residence can be purchased with 5% down. However, there is a program called "Second Home" that people can use to purchase another property that they could use and only require a minimum of 5% down payment. Some people use these programs to purchase recreational property that they use or another home closer to their employment (if they had to work out of town). Some parents even use these programs to purchase a home far from the parental home for their children to live in while the children attend school. In theory, you can actually own two properties with only 5% down payment. There are strict requirements and qualifications that I would not go into details about. It is best to contact me directly or another mortgage broker for details. At the time of writing this book, CMHC (Canadian Mortgage Housing Corporation) has already closed this program and only Genworth or Canada Guaranty still offers it. I am certain things will tighten up even more as the years go by and the remaining two insurers may eventually follow CMHC's lead.

If someone in the above scenario has already taken advantage of the 5% down primary and second home program, can he or she purchase another property with 5% down payment? The official answer is also NO. I thought that was the case myself until I came across a client that had a unique situation and purchased his third home with 5% down payment. Let's call him Bob. Bob was a highly paid executive that had to occasionally relocate every few years due to his occupation. He contacted me to help him with refinancing one of his properties. He had already purchased his 2 homes with 5% down earlier in his career. During his last relocation he decided that he did not want to sell his primary residence just in case he wanted to move back to the city. He decided to rent it out and told his bank about his situation. He was able to purchase his new property which became his "new primary residence" and was only required to put down 5% as down payment on the new property. At the time of writing this book, this option is on the verge of facing extinction as well. However, as long as the first property has more than 20% equity, you can expect to purchase the next property with a minimum 5% down payment again. This program may also be affected in the near future.

Passing the Buck

CMHC, Genworth and Canada Guaranty are the three big players that offer default insurance to the lenders for high ratio mortgages. When someone wants to purchase a house but has less than 20% for a down payment, then most likely that person will have to pay for default insurance in order to receive financing for the purchase of that property. It was made extremely popular by the media's constant barrage of 5% down or 0% down marketing over the years. Many people in the industry will tell you that you could get lower interest on a mortgage as long as you contribute less than 20% down payment towards your purchase. This is a fact.

This little-known fact encouraged a lot of professionals in the industry to "recommend" their client to put less than 20% towards their down payment just to qualify for the lower rate on their mortgage. Clients loved it since they could brag to their friends and family how low their mortgage rates were, and the brokers also won an easy client. It was mostly prevalent in the mortgage broker side of the industry, but the retail banks quickly learned about this tactic and quickly jumped on the band wagon. When the major banks started using the same strategy as the brokerage houses, it accelerated the risks that CMHC has taken on. The potential liabilities to the taxpayer quickly skyrocketed and pushed CMHC into the spotlight. Our government reacted as fast as it could during the years of 2008 to 2014 by making numerous changes to regulate the market and control the growing risk but to no avail; the market continues to grow.

The government put a stop to zero-percent-down financing because of the growing risk of a similar meltdown as the United States. Even though most lenders have stopped promoting "0% down" programs to purchase a home, you can still do it. Most banks found a creative loophole and would be able to give you a personal credit line or term loan for the 5% and finance the remaining 95%, which would be backed by the insurers. As long as the client has sufficient high income, any broker or mortgage specialist would be able to help finance the purchase with zero money down.

Power Games: Who's Got the Ball?

I must give a hand to the banks out there because they know their strengths and weaknesses and have focused their money on having the public only focus on their strengths. The main strength that the brick and mortar (aka retail bank) lenders have is the convenience and ability to offer multiple services and products to keep you loyal to them. Do you know they have major weaknesses that people do not realize or pay attention to? Most people don't realize this, but they have contributed to their record profits year after year. Banks do not offer what is best for you but rather what is most profitable for them and their shareholders. I know most people realize this, but do you really understand how or why?

It's all about control. The bank's primary objective is to control the ball. You are the ball. The more they wrap their fingers around you by convincing you to buy more services and products from them, the more entangled you are. This will make it much more difficult for you to leave them, thus giving the bank more control of your financial life. They will do everything and say absolutely anything to keep you in their claws. They will even unjustifiably slander the competition just to keep your business.

Financial institutions have developed tactics and strategies to lock you in and prevent you from going elsewhere. Refinancing or renewing your mortgage is a great example. Getting an appraisal done for financing is usually ordered by the lender, but the client usually pays for that expense. Clients end up paying for it but cannot use it at their discretion. If the lender decides not to offer the financing, the client will have to pay for another appraisal to be done at the new bank. If the appraisal shows that the property has fallen short of expectation due to certain criteria that were conditioned on the loan, that's money wasted. The client cannot request that the appraisal be used by a different lender since the bank had ordered it. In the eyes of the appraisal company, the bank is the actual client and not the applicant/borrower. The bank will not give the client permission to use it for another lender. The client will have to order another appraisal and pay for it again, even if it is with the same appraisal company. To you and me, this is a totally unfair and unjust practice. I know. It's unbelievable that this practice is allowed to happen.

It doesn't have to be that way. If a mortgage broker orders an appraisal on behalf of the client to give to the lender that has conditioned it, the mortgage broker should be able to use that same appraisal for a different lender if the first lender decides not to commit to the financing they had originally offered. Now you have control of your own ball in your own court. Why do you think that the banks are afraid of mortgage brokers? We give control back to the consumer, and that is something they do not want to lose.

Mistake #1: Not Knowing Your Mortgage Type

In mortgage financing, there is an ongoing battle for control. Most people are not aware that the type of registration on the title of their property is the way the banks win control. In Canada and many places around the world, there are two ways to register a mortgage at the land title office: Standard mortgages and collateral charge mortgages. What's the big deal, you may ask? For one, a standard mortgage is simply whatever you borrow; they register that amount against the property. When you need to move to a new bank, the new bank just changes the name of the mortgage lender on that document. The amount owed can be easily ascertained. It would be a very quick and inexpensive process for the new lender. However, if the existing lender has registered it as a collateral charge, the amount owed is unknown and cannot be determined by looking up the land title registration.

In a collateral charge mortgage, the only document registered at the title office directs anyone to go to the existing lender to request for the details of that mortgage. In the majority of cases, the existing lender will actually register an amount much greater than what you had borrowed. In many circumstances, the registered amount could be as high as 125% of the value of the property or more. I know this does not make much common sense. Why would anyone knowingly want to have that registered against their property?

Many customers don't realize this and unwittingly have their mortgages registered this way. Now, I am not against this type of mortgage registration. For the right client or investor, it may be a great strategy, but doing it across the board for everyone is not good. Many who were aware that they were registering a much higher amount on their property than what they borrowed and allowed to do it were most likely sold on it. In other words, the "sales associate" or bank employee had convinced the clients that it was good. They usually do this by telling customers that they can access more funds at a later date without going to a lawyer and incurring legal expense. Not requiring a lawyer will potentially save the client a few hundred dollars. The customer can come back to borrow more and more when the value of their home goes up. Sounds great doesn't it? Well what's the catch?

Mistake #2: Not Asking the Right Questions

The customer isn't warned that he or she will be required to have their credit checked at a future date when the customer comes back to request additional funds. Most people only need to borrow more money when times are tough or if they have had something bad happen in their life. If at that time, any material changes that the customer has made or been affected by since the last credit check (such as loss of employment or a decreased credit score from late payments etc), the lender will not advance any further funds. They would have to go elsewhere to get the loan. This is where the problem pops up. I have encountered many clients over the years that have fallen into this situation. If you were that customer, your problem is exacerbated even further since you are in dire need of money and your mortgage is registered as a collateral charge.

How is that you ask? When clients come to see me or another lender for additional funds, we will check the existing title registration. Even though the existing lender will not advance anymore funds due to the client's current situation, the way that a collateral charge is registered tells the potential private lender that the existing bank may extend more credit (even if it won't). It will show that the current lender can potentially advance more funds up to 125% of the property value. If the new lender extends any funds, they would be in second priority on the property. In a loan default situation, the first lender would get paid out first and the second lender may end up with nothing. Would you as a private lender want to risk lending any money behind that fact? This is primarily why I do not support this type of mortgage registration to be given to every customer.

As you can see, in a collateral charge mortgage, the customer loses control of his ability to secure any future financing. He literally relinquishes that to the bank by signing on the dotted line without asking what type of registration will be used on their mortgage. He would need to go to another lender to receive the loan and pay off the existing lender entirely. This process will incur a stiff penalty and more expense to redo the registration on the legal documents into a standard mortgage. Ironically, a client agrees to a collateral mortgage to save money, but it will cost him more money in the future. So really, only the bank wins by doing this since it makes it costly for you to leave the bank or get funds elsewhere. You have no control over your mortgage when it is a collateral charge mortgage. When you need it most, it won't be of any help. A collateral mortgage saving you money is a bold-faced lie. Understand what you are signing away.

If you must get a mortgage from a lender that only has a collateral agreement registered on your property, make sure that you have a say in what the amount is to be registered. Always opt to only register the amount that you are borrowing from them. It does not make any sense to register more than what you borrow and even less to register it over 100% of your property value. You will be tying your property up and may not be able to access any equity if your personal financial situation is affected in the future. Play it smart and keep control of your debt instead of relinquishing that right to the lender.

Making the Most of the Foreclosure Blues

Always Pay the Piper

Everyone have good days and bad days; just don't let one bad day ruin your life. If you are "in arrears" -- generally described as having missed three monthly payments — the bank can initiate a power of sale against you and put your property on the market. Most people know this as "foreclosure." If your home sells for less than your loan, you're still on the hook for any debt outstanding plus legal fees for many years after. That's a pretty scary situation.

If and when you are in a financially tough situation, let your lender know. It is a myth that the banks like to foreclose on people and take away their home. The opposite is actually truer. Banks are in the business of lending and that's all they want to do. Many lenders will have provisions that may allow you to legitimately skip payments or be able to use up your previous pre-payments to go towards future monthly payments. There are life events (such as terminal illness or disability) that may also qualify for assistance from government agencies to help intervene.

Just remember, it's not over until it's over. Even if it seems there is no way out of your financial situation, go find an independent mortgage broker. They should be able to help you and give you a lease on life and time to put your financial house in order. Independent mortgage brokers have much more access to different types of lenders.

You Can Take That to the Bank!

The act of going through a foreclosure actually costs the lenders a lot of time and money. They actually lose more by going through the process than you would think. They have to hire outside professionals to do all the extra work. It may seem that they get their money back, but in reality, it is far from the truth. They incur legal (conveyance and court time) expense, realtor expense and many other associated costs. The foreclosure process is not a simple one, and it takes many months to complete the process. Sometimes it could drag on for more than a year or two. The human resources required to keep track of each foreclosure cost the bank dearly. Most often, the bank does not recoup the money they loaned out since foreclosed properties are usually sold under market value. To add insult to injury, they now lose a client for life, and the lender's reputation is negatively affected. Anyone in the client's circle of influence would hear the story about the bad bank foreclosing on their good friend. "That's great and all, but how does this help me?" you ask. Understand this industry secret, and you may end up being the winner still.

A great saying that I have heard since my childhood comes to mind, "Knowing is half the battle." Armed with this knowledge, you can leverage that to your advantage rather than feeling like a pawn in the game of life. You have a great advantage if you are transparent with the lender and approach them early on. Most lenders will rather work with you and do everything in their power to find a way to help you with your temporary financial situation rather than foreclose on you. Lenders would rather let you sell the property or find an alternate way to pay them than put you into a court order sale. "Why?" you may ask. This way they won't incur any added expense. They're not Mother Theresa, but what they do know is that if they can help you, you won't think so badly about them, and they get to protect their reputation. It is not just financially in their best interest to help you but a great strategy for long- term customer retention. Even if you no longer have a mortgage with them, you will continue to use their other services and buy other products. Talk about loyal for life!

If things don't work out, at least you get to control how the sale of your property is played out. When customers ignore the lenders and the bank itself takes ownership of the asset (your property), you will have very little recourse in court. However, if you were up front with them and did everything to fix the situation but still end up not being able to make payments, you will still have the upper hand. The court will handle the foreclosure and if any money remains after the sale, you will get to keep it. If the same thing had happened and you had ignored the bank, they can take over ownership of the property and dispose of it. In that situation, they will be able to sell your property and keep any profit.

As you can see, you can still come up the winner of a bad situation if you know the rules of engagement. As in poker, a losing hand can still make you a winner.

Know Your Investor

Be Wary of the Yes Man

Incompetence and greed are found in every industry, and the financial industry is not lacking of those people, either. The mortgage industry is full of hungry wolves going after the same thing, new business. Many of them would say yes to everything that is asked of them just to get the client's business. Just like a slave. "Yes, master". Many overpromise and under deliver. Many don't even deliver. I've seen it happen before me many times over the years and heard about it countless more times from unhappy clients. Some clients were even angry about the whole experience.

Clients only want one thing. They want results or a quick reply that it is not possible. Clients don't want to be dragged around for weeks or months. Sometimes things happen beyond the control of the advisor. Clients will understand. The advisor just needs to keep the client aware of the situation, keep in constant contact, and update the client as the days go by. This is maintaining trust and building a long-term relationship. However, most advisors miss this whole point entirely. They're afraid that if they have no answer or a negative answer, the clients will go elsewhere or lose faith in them. Sadly, the opposite is truer. Only the two percent-ers (2%'er) understand this philosophy and make it a core part of their business practice. They succeed in good or bad times. I believe I do my best to stay in this category. People are people, and we are all the same under the skin. We all have a heart and bleed the same way. It's not rocket science. They will understand, and it is okay to say "No."

Jack-of-All-Trades and Master of None

There are two main types of advisors in this industry; the expert and the jack-of-all-trades. An expert is someone who specializes in a particular area and excels at what he does. A Jack-of-all-trades is somewhat good at everything but not particular great at it. There is nothing bad about generalists in certain fields, at least the ones that deal with minor amounts of money. However, it is quite dangerous to enlist a generalist when you are dealing with millions of dollars. A minor mistake can be cost hundreds of thousands, if not millions.

I specialize in commercial financing because it is what I do best, and I love it. I understand the complexity and enjoy the challenge. Solving the financial challenge in commercial financing is very rewarding. Not just financially but mentally. There is a great sense of accomplishment, knowing that not everyone can do it and because it requires a lot of thinking and creativity to come up with a solution. It also requires me to tap my network of all the relationships I have built over the years. Every lender has his flavor of the day, and that flavor changes from month to month and year to year. Staying in touch and keeping those connections is sometimes the key to solving a financial problem for my client.

I love everyone in my industry and have no ill feelings toward them. There is a lot of money to go around if we only focus on helping our client. First and foremost, each finance professional should have your best interest at heart. I am saddened when I come across an unhappy client due to greed or malice. It makes me wonder why it happens so often. If the advisors were smart enough to know that they're not smart enough to do the job, they should call someone for assistance or refer that business to an expert. The sad reality is that most are hungry wolves. They are willing to undertake a task even if they are fully aware that they are inept at it. Why do they do it? I don't have all the answers but can only guess that they have selfish reasons. When I am overwhelmed with business and new clients inquire, I don't accept the business and usually refer it to another broker. I can take the application or contact information and explain to the client that it would be in his or her best interest to have someone else take care of it. Someone else that can dedicate the time that is necessary for a successful outcome. They respect me and refer me future business, as well as referring their friends and family. Everyone wins when I set aside my personal agenda and instead focus on what would be best for these potential clients.

What many mortgage advisors do not realize in the industry is that by being selfish and greedy, they only hurt themselves. A strong and successful future in the business is based upon referrals and repeat business. If you have to forever go out and hunt for the next "meal ticket," you are heading for failure. The secret to longevity is building on existing clientele and helping them improve their financial situation. The more we help our clients, the more we will also reap the rewards.

Psychology of a Client or Investor

The more we understand each other, the better everything around us seems to become. What are clients are afraid of or should they be afraid of? A few important issues come to mind. Once you put yourself in the other person's shoes and think as they would, your chances of doing business with that person increase exponentially.

• **Trustworthiness?** Is the person you are interviewing to become your advisor someone that you will want to work with you for many years to come? The biggest concern that any clients have is, "Is this person looking out for my best interest or his pocket book?" Is there a chance for conflict of interest? If that does happen, who will that advisor truly represent? You or his employer?

• **Integrity**? Does this person have integrity; does he or she ask for extra money or offer to forge your documents for a price? Does he or she convince you to mislead the lender on the application to get it financed?

• **Good deal?** Is this the best deal that I can possibly get? What happens if the rate/price drops later? Can I get out of that contract without any expense?

• **Free ride?** What are the hidden costs or potential hidden expenses? If it's too good to be true, get independent legal advice. If the advisor does not suggest that, find a different one.

There is No Shortcut in Life

Beware of anyone that will tell you he can get you financing 100% guaranteed. Fraud-Alert. There is no easy way to get money. Even if you are an unwitting participant, the bank will revoke the loan if you are deemed to have received the funds via fraudulent means. There are many unscrupulous bank employees and independent mortgage brokers in the industry. Be warned. There is no such thing as a free ride.

The repercussions are unimaginable if you are found to be involved in fraudulent financing. It won't matter if you are an unknowing participant. Even in those situations, the loan may be called and you will have to locate alternate lenders or face foreclosure. If you did not qualify for a loan previously and your situation has not improved, you may be in for a very bad experience.

If you know the broker or advisor has a bad reputation or "good" reputation for being able to finance everything with 100% guarantee, you should do some homework first. Our parents always told us that if it sounds too good to be true, it probably is. They did not say that to make us worry warts but to make us to more aware of things and make us use our brain more often.

If it sounds too good to be true, be warned; there is no shortcut in financing.

The Mortgage Broker's Secret Weapon (and Kryptonite)

Many people in my industry will not like what I have to share. It's our secret weapon that allows us to beat the banks in the rate war. As every super hero is told, "With great power comes great responsibility." Our access to such a diverse range of lenders across the country and their stable of products provides independent brokers an unfair advantage over individual banks that have a limited product line.

On top of that, mortgage brokers have a secret weapon. With this weapon, they can beat most of their competition. They can do it because they have discretion to use their commission to "buy down" the rate. It's an industry term which means that a broker can trade a percentage of his or her earnings to lower the rate from the chosen lender for the client. Theoretically they can use up all their commissions to beat any bank rate by a good margin. They would also be poor and starving.

I'm not a fan of using the rate buy down. There are several reasons, but the main one is that I believe a broker's job is much more than just offering the lowest rate to win a customer over. It is an important factor but should not be the only determining factor to work with a mortgage broker. I believe in a win-win-win arrangement. When a broker has to end up on the losing side by buying down the rate to win the client, what does it say about the client? It's a win-lose for the broker. Importantly, what does that say about the mortgage broker? Does the broker not have sufficient competence to value himself enough to earn the wages that he deserves? Would you as a client feel confident in the broker's experience or skill about future financing situations that are not straight forward? I would bet the answer would be no.

I have only done that once when I first started in the business many years ago. I can tell you how I felt afterwards. It wasn't good. I felt like I was a street beggar that was willing to settle for any scraps of food and felt like I was desperate. I was neither. Even worse, I felt that the client didn't see any value in my knowledge or expertise and that the client didn't care how that affected me. Did it make me feel that I should value that client as a highly valuable and important person that deserves my advice over the years? No. I did not. I didn't like that client at all. Did I want to feel that way about my clients? No. I did not. I wanted to be a trusted advisor so that whenever my clients call, I will be their best friend and be excited to hear from them. I want to be grateful that they're still calling me for advice many years later. This is what I wanted.

I had a dilemma on my hands. How would I want to be treated if I were my own client? How can I treat everyone as if they were my own family? What if my father became my client? How should I treat him? I made a decision that day that I would never devalue myself or my service again. I would earn my pay and give more than enough to deserve the money. This way I would be very happy to help and offer advice that is truly in their best interest whenever they talk to me. If you were my client, which choice would you rather have?

A race to the bottom, putting price as the most important factor in a decision making process would only lead to one thing: Someone loses. Everybody wants to win, right? When one party loses, there is no longer good will towards each other. When all parties at the table win, everyone is happy and each is more than willing to go out of his or her way to help the other. Wouldn't you want that?

Nobody Wins in the Race to the Bottom

Some people abuse the relationship between a mortgage broker and a bank mortgage advisor in order to get the best rate possible even though there is more value than getting the best rate or best mortgage product by using a mortgage broker over a bank employee. There is one big common dirty secret that a mortgage broker and the bank mortgage advisor have. They don't like to admit it, but both are active players on both sides of the playing field. Some unscrupulous customers will approach a mortgage broker to get them the best rate possible and then use that mortgage quote against the bank representative to beat the mortgage broker's rate.

If the client has a high net worth or profitable client, the bank will match or beat the broker rate just to retain the client. The dirty secret is that the bank does not see the interest earned on the mortgage as a profit vehicle. The real money is made on the back end. They know from statistics that over 40% of mortgage holders will encounter a life event before the term is up and will incur the stiff penalty that mortgages have. This is one of the bank's largest contributor to their record quarterly profit. It is a rotten thing to take advantage of a mortgage broker, but some lenders do it. I am not here to tell you whether that is right or wrong. Some would say there is nothing wrong since it is just business. I am sure most if not all mortgage brokers would disagree though.

Perhaps this may be a blessing in disguise for mortgage brokers. These are not the type of clients that you would want to have around for your entire career anyway. They will drain you mentally and physically with their demands and for the amount of time spent on them, you can make more money serving clients that you enjoy having. As a mortgage broker, you will never bend over backwards to help these rate-driven clients. You will go the extra mile for the ones that are willing to pay you what your time is worth. These rate-driven clients are considered undesirable clients in the industry for a reason. If they do this at the start of the relationship with you, they are sure to do the same thing again once their mortgage is up for renewal. Want a repeat of it again in a few years? I doubt it. Don't ever worry about letting the banks win these types of client. It can be spiritually rewarding just to let them go. Take my word for it.

It is better to focus all your energy and time on the clients that value your time and do not ask you for discounts or for you to lower your fees. If your fees are reasonable and you give them more value than they expect, they will accept your fees as fair. Go above and beyond for these clients. Remember their anniversary, their kid's birthday and give them meaningful gifts over the years. They in turn will bring you more clients like themselves. Put most of your marketing budget into giving back to those clients who support you in your business rather than spending it on advertising.

Things That Make You Go "Hmmm?"

The stories that I hear over the years could make you laugh, cry and sometimes shock you. Every now and then I hear the "*100% guaranteed you're approved*" nightmares. Sometimes I end up fixing those so called mobile mortgage advisor loans or bank manager loans that had guaranteed 100% approval before even submitting the application. It's not because these customers are gullible or blissfully ignorant. If you are a current client of that bank, they have an internal credit scoring system that gives them an idea of credit worthiness and most often the advisors based their "quick" decisions on those merits alone. When it is time to make an active request for a large loan, they have to check and update the clients' financials from the central credit bureau. When the report comes back bad, this is where those *100% guaranteed* applications fall apart.

Sometimes it's not about the client's bad financial situation. Sometimes they are the unwitting pawns of fraud. I am not the only advisor that has heard these stories.

Fraud committed by customers is easy to spot. Fraud created by industry insiders is much more difficult to spot. Aside from the professional fraudsters, there are three types of people that have an easier time achieving financing through fraudulent means. Disgruntled bank employees, greedy advisors (bank or independent brokers) and friends or relatives of the first two groups. My point in this section is to warn potential fraudsters that they will be caught, and no matter what their reasoning is, it is not worth it. These are only my opinions and should not be construed as facts. I do not know the exact statistics and am only writing this to inform the base about what I hear, read and observe.

Short-Term Gain for Long-Term Pain...

The first group, the disgruntled bank employee is much easier to spot and catch. They just don't know it. Most are careless and not professional fraudsters. The computer systems that the bank's operation centers use are vastly more powerful than last year's super computers. They have software with highly intelligent algorithms to actively search and flag fraudulent applications and log as proof. Whatever the reason is for doling out loans and credit that customers should not qualify for, it is not worth the jail time or getting a criminal conviction over. Getting fired should be the least of their concern. You hear the stories in the media every now and then. They always get caught. Every keystroke performed on a bank's computer system is monitored and tracked nowadays. If they're thinking about doing it to spite their employer, it isn't worth it. They will get caught and I guarantee you that nobody will be laughing.

Mobile specialists or independent mortgage brokers are the most creative of the group and most motivated to actively or passively commit fraud on behalf of the client. Now, let me clarify that I am not suggesting this happens often, just that it has in the past and it most likely will happen somewhere to some lender in the future. I know for a fact that it is happening in our city today and most likely every city across the country. How do I know this? I have had potential clients approaching me over the years asking if I could help them "write up false documents" to help them get financing. Some of them even offered me money as a bribe. I am certain if it's happening to me, it must be happening to others.

This year alone, on two separate occasions, I was asked if I would help them. One recent client I turned down asked me if I knew and could refer them to the person in the East Indian community that is helping other people get guaranteed financing. I am not saying that the East Indian community is doing it en masse. Just that I know someone in that community is doing it. It is shortsighted to risk one's career for short-term pay. Sure, a person can make decent money by doing it but once caught (and he or she will be caught), that person will be banned for a very long time from the entire financial industry. Having a criminal history will also affect many other types of employment and forever close off many future opportunities. Is all the pain and grief worth the few thousand dollars one would receive by committing these crimes? Not for me, thank you.

The third group is the one that upsets me the most. These are the so-called family members or good friends that abuse their relationship with the advisor/broker to put a fraudulent application through the system. I nearly became the pawn of a fraudulent loan early in my career. A distant relative of the family was in need of refinancing. I believed they were good people and since they were relatives, I dropped my guard that time. Everything they gave me,

I accepted at face value and submitted to it without carefully going over it as I usually do. When the credit department that reviewed the application and documents contacted me about a forged document, I was stunned. Thank God, I had a very good relationship with the person that notified me of this. Just to make a long story short. I told that relative to go elsewhere. I wouldn't help him any further. He is also no longer on my trusted list. He nearly cost me my career. I don't care what the intention was. I don't have much respect for people that abuse a professional's position. It was a hard lesson to learn but it made me a much keener person in regard to compliance and fraud.

People don't realize it but it is not just a serious crime in itself, but the repercussions go farther than that single event. The fallout of fraud is huge. If I did not have trust and a relationship established with that lender, I would not have been able to remain in the finance industry.

Whether you had an active or passive role in the fraud itself, the bank has the right to call the loan. If the fraud was caught and committed by an insider, the lenders would have gone through every single loan that the advisor or employee made in the past. They would check every single customer and question the qualification. If any approved loans are found that should not have qualified, they would be in serious jeopardy.

If you did not qualify for the loan legally, the bank has the authority to ask for full repayment. Being forced out of your home in the middle of winter would not be fun. Being ignorant will not make your situation any better. Just remember, if it's too good to be true, it probably is. The next time someone tells you that he or she can guarantee your loan approval, should you be happy or worried? Use some common sense and run the other way.

Putting All Your Eggs in One Basket

Many financial advisors will tell you that putting all your investments in one place is a very bad idea. They say it's the worst investment decision you could ever make. Most people generally agree and avoid doing that. The funny thing is that the same people usually have their entire banking needs done at one bank. Isn't that like putting all your eggs in one basket? Isn't there a risk involved in doing that? Most people don't see the inherent risk of this choice and justify that decision by saying they are creating long-term relationships.

"What could be the potential risk," you might ask? Let me ask you, "What would happen if that bank does something that really upsets you, and you never want to deal with them ever again?" How much time and grief would it take to move your business elsewhere? Is it even possible if you have a business that is so interconnected to that bank for incoming deposits or payments? They would really have you at their mercy then, wouldn't they?

If you or someone you know is currently in that situation, you should really sit down and rethink your situation and regain control by diversifying your banking needs. Having long-term relationships with multiple lenders will allow you to easily continue your business with fewer interruptions if you are ever caught in a situation that makes you want to cut ties with a particular bank.

There are many other benefits from diversifying such as having more access to different products, services, locations, servicing hours, deposit guarantees and advisors with different expertise.

Mortgage Brokers' Secrets

Are you a broker that wants a never-ending stream of referrals but are afraid to get out of your comfort zone? I can help you to have fun and enjoy getting out of your comfort zone to achieve that goal. Can you imagine what it would be like if you could approach anyone anywhere and engage them in what you have to offer?

Let me ask you some questions. When you know the answers to these, you can become a successful mortgage broker. Once you know the answer to these questions, you will thrive:

- What are mortgage brokers afraid of or should be afraid of?
- Do you know enough about what the client really needs to truly help them? How can you get them to really open up to share with you the one thing that will make them your lifelong client?
- Are you playing as you go or are you calling in for help from a mentor? Will your client leave you if he or she recognizes that you don't know your stuff? As a rule of thumb, being transparent has always won me more loyalty points than pretending I know everything when I don't. When I encounter a client that asks questions that I do not immediately know the answer to, I would tell them that it is a great question, and I would have to get back to them on that. Then I'd make a note and do so.
- Is this a rate shopper that will waste your time? How can I prevent being "shopped"? What questions should I ask to find out the level of commitment my potential client has with me if I do all this work to get him the best deal possible?
- Are you at the mercy of an underwriter (to make exception or not). Do you understand enough about the client to sell the client to the lender as a win-win deal?
- How will you win clients that have no intention of giving you the business unless you get better rates than their bank?

55

I have been involved in the financial services industry for over 15 years. I have learned what works, what doesn't work, what to say, when and how to say it to get the deal done. I have found a secret formula that has helped me as a mortgage broker to grow my business massively. I went from being an average income earner to tripling my income in less than 18 months. I can share with you the 15 key things that have contributed to my massive growth in the business in such a short time. Whether you are an advisor, sales person, or sub-contractor, you can use my formula to achieve massive success in your business.

My passion in life is helping others to achieve great success in their life as I have in mine. Many people have directly and indirectly helped me along my journey to success and I am eternally grateful. I would like to give back. My biggest dream is to help other entrepreneurs on their journey. The day I stopped worrying about money and focused on my clients was the day it seemed as if the Universe was driving people to my door; the opportunities kept coming and knocking at my door. I am so grateful and I want to give back to help improve the industry. I want to help make the profession become more respected. I hope this book helps change the way professionals in the industry think and do business. If you feel that you could use my help on your success journey, I will be honored to help you.

Questions You Should Have Asked

Everyone knows the usual questions that are frequently asked such as rates, terms, amortizations, and closing costs (legal fees, transfer taxes etc). People don't ask the more important questions, the scary stuff...the questions that they SHOULD ask, but do not.

- Is my pre-approval 100% approved for financing to remove subjects on my offer to purchase?
- Is the final commitment letter, a guarantee that my mortgage has been completed? Even after documents have been signed at the lawyer's office, the lender still has the right to cancel that commitment if he or she deems or suspects any sign of fraud (proven or not). It rarely happens, but it does happen.
- If my financial situation falls apart and affects my credit, can I get assurance that I can access the equity in my home?
- What will happen if a life event happens and I can't pay for a while? Is there anything I can do or prepare in advance? What options do I have available to me?
- Can I withdraw money that I had previously prepaid (annual pre-payment)?
- If my marriage falls apart, what options are available to me?
- Can I sell my home to a relative or family member to get out of a mortgage?

A competent and knowledgeable broker should know all the answers to these critical questions. He should bring it to his client's attention whether or not his client asks about it.

How to Become the Go-To Expert

15 Secrets to Your Success

What I am about to share with you is something personal to me. These words are based on my experience, my view, and my own opinion. My success only came once I had matured in the industry. Maturity came to me not from getting older but rather from a change in mindset and clarity that I have gained in my brief time in this industry.

When you apply what I have learned as I show you in this book, it will fundamentally change the way you think about your finances and how you do business with people in the industry. Your perception of clients – professional relationships and how to treat others will forever change. You will find opportunities in places you would have never thought possible, and those opportunities will come to you more frequently.

The following are fifteen lessons, ideas and simple ingredients that have helped to fuel my current success as a mortgage broker:

Secret # 1

- **Your core belief**. I am a big believer of Karma and what goes around comes around. I have lived long enough to see what greed can do and how many lives it can damage. I have also seen what good Karma can bring. Until you've seen both sides of the finished picture, it's hard to fully understand it. Yes, I know that hearing this is no solace for people who have been taken advantage of. Karma is nothing to jest about, though. I have seen many people from my past that has done wrong to other people. Those people have been punished severely compared to their acts or misdeeds. Payback is a "bitch" if you're on the receiving end of it.

Take my word for it. Be good, do good, and just like a long-term investment, it will compound, and you will reap the eventual payoffs. You'll be glad you did it.

Integrity is everything. This is a core belief that I value most. My father was a perfect role model of that. His word was his bond. Neither poor weather nor being ill would prevent him from showing up when he said he would. Nobody would even consider if he had ulterior motives when he did something or asked someone to do something for him. I am glad that everything I do and the decisions I make must fit in with my core belief. My deceased father would not have liked it any other way.

I believe that **family must come first**. My client's family and my family should always take priority over business. If and when I am faced with a question about money or a business decision, I would always look at how it would affect my client's family or mine. If it affects only my client's family, I would ask myself, "Would my family be happy with the decision I am about to make?" If it only affects me or my family, I ask the very same question. Nothing in my life should ever supersede a family's life.

Everyone's a winner baby! It was part of a song I heard a long time ago when I was in high school. I loved it and it has been a part of my life for a very long time. It's quite funny how a small thing like that can affect you and how things turn out. The business world always used a phrase that everyone should have a "win-win" attitude. The two parties to any transaction should have a positive outcome for each side. For a long time, that was how I saw it too. When I entered the financial services industry, it opened my eyes to a third party. I did not realize it, but when we only focus on ourselves and the client, we are missing the third person. The supplier or connector should be a part of the win-win solution as well. I believe that when we are dealing with people, we should consider a "win-win-win" outcome. There is always a third person involved. Whether that third part is a silent partner or not, he or she too deserves to win just as much as we do. This may not make much sense right now, but give it some thought and reflect on your past transactions. Think about how you could have done things differently and allow the third party to win just as much as the two primary people involved. Could it have improved your relationship with that person or company? Could you have leveraged that relationship even better if you had done so? Now can you see how a "win-win-win" attitude could be more beneficial than just a "win-win" attitude?

These are my three core beliefs. I believe these are important ingredients that helped me achieve my current level of success. I know that it will take me to the next level in my business and family life.

Secret # 2

- **"Change is good and everything happens for a reason."**
Nothing ever happens by mistake. Mistakes happen but not for no reason. These are the words of wisdom that have helped me through the "tough times" of my life and helped me through my career transition from the computer industry to financial services. It was a difficult decision leaving the career that I dreamed of doing when I was a kid. It was a defining moment when I realized that I was miserable doing what I was doing. I knew right then and there that I had to make a drastic change. I did not even ponder the cost of time and money that I had spent to get to where I was at that time. I just felt it was time, and I had to make up my mind. Now or never. Looking back, I can say that I made the right decision. It was the hardest decision I have ever made. I didn't know why or what it was that made me decide to make a big change. It was one of those defining moments. It just felt right. Many similar moments will occur in your life, just have faith that change is good.

Secret # 3

- **Never overpromise and under deliver.** It's a bad way to do business. Companies should present the truth and reality of the industry to newcomers rather than give false hope and create unreal expectations. When I first joined a mortgage company, I was told that they would get me leads and that on average I should expect one every 2 or 3 months. I was told that there were leads that come through the office or website that would be fairly distributed to each sub-broker and then shared with every member. I can say that I had zero referrals from our office during the two years that I was with them. Lesson for newcomers: don't buy into every marketing hype that they tell you. The lesson that I learned from this experience was to tell all my new brokers how tough it is out there and what it would take to make it in this industry. I tell it like it is and since we're all adults, there is no need to flower it up or pull punches. The only promise I make is to provide the tools to help each member get to where he or she would like to be. Treat your clients exactly the same way you would want to be treated and over-deliver!

Secret # 4

- **Be prepared and be strategic.** Feast or famine cycle is what most commission professionals experience when they are new to the industry. One month you will do very well, and the next month you will go hungry because you have no clients. This is a reality that most sales professionals and entrepreneurs face when they are new. Many fail because they were not made aware of the reality and what they thought would happen did not match their expectations. People wanting to pursue their dream of running their own business eventually fail because of unreal expectations and not enough preparation for the long journey. My advice to many budding entrepreneurs and rising stars in the financial industry is to be prepared for a marathon. Put your house in order by having two to three years' worth of savings to supplement your income or having credit lines available that would allow you time to build your business. It is not that you won't make money, but you will certainly underestimate the expenses that will add up as you run your business. Most business will take two to three years to grow large enough to achieve a steady income. Therefore, success is for those who persevere and last long enough to reap the harvest. Like a marathon, entering this business is not for those that are impatient and want instant gratification. That's a short sprint. You will burn out and die a quick but painful death.

Nobody likes the get rich slow strategy. Most prefer the get rich quick method. The statistics on failures from those businesses is staggering but many prefer to take that route. Guess what the success statistics are for those that are on the get rich slow method? You guessed it, much higher than zero. Be prepared for the long haul, and you will achieve your goal.

Secret # 5

- **Never burn your bridges.** "To err is human; to forgive, divine." Whatever you do, never, ever burn your bridges, your partners, clients or suppliers. Never! An entire workshop should be taught on why how and what to do to maintain relationships. We all make mistakes, and if we own up to it and ask for forgiveness, amazing things can happen. I can share with you many stories about some of my abysmal failures that I have turned into great success stories. People are not stupid, and I don't believe any of my clients or potential clients were. I am sure yours are the same. Why then do most of us treat other people like they are dumb and won't know when we make mistakes? I recognized early on that whenever I fail someone or in some way, I need to correct that mistake and take ownership. Several circumstances that nearly resulted in becoming stories of failure were resolved quickly and won me those same clients for life. I can speak from experience that failure is not failure but a sign that I need to make a change in my course direction. If something bad happens, I review it afterwards, learn from it, and move on. Failure is only fatal if you don't learn anything from it.

Secret # 6

- **Don't bite the hands that feed you.** Be good to your partners and suppliers. Respect them. Take what our parents taught us: "If you don't have anything nice to say, don't say it." Saying something mean or in spite would only hurt the relationship. You may need the relationship one day, and you will never get a favor done if your relationship has been tainted by a single incident in the past. You can do 999 good things and do 1 bad thing. Guess what people remember you by? Unfortunately, that one bad thing will come to mind first. This happens during conversation due to misunderstandings, misinformation or just plainly misinterpretation of the meaning. Much can be corrected during live interactions, but most relationships are damaged due to email correspondence or social media posting/messaging. The one rule that has saved me from making more erroneous judgments and misunderstandings was to wait 24 hours or at least half a day before replying to something that was emotionally charged. We are human beings and as humans, our strength and weakness are the same. Emotions are critical for deep relationships, but they are also a source of great pain when used incorrectly. Our parents were right, watch what you say or you will regret it one day. This also applies to what we do on the internet. I make it a rule, and it has saved me countless times from further self-inflicted pain.

Secret # 7

- **Work hard but don't ever lose the farm.** In my first 2 years I worked harder and harder and my daily work hours increased accordingly. My income grew 50% in the 2nd year, but so did the amount of hours I spent in my business and away from my family. I had reasoned that I was only working harder to increase my income so that I can take better care of my family and children. At one point, I was seeing less and less of my wife and kids. I was only able to kiss them good night, and most of the time they were already fast asleep when I got home. One day my wife asked me why I was working so hard. I told her that I wanted to give my kids the future that I never had. I wanted to provide for them and give them better things in life than I had when I was young. I wanted to have everything in place so that they need not worry about their future. I still remember that day vividly. She asked me, "How much time have my daughters seen me during their waking hours." At that moment, I felt as if I was ripped and shaken from a bad nightmare. I did not realize I was travelling on the same path my father had. The very same thing that I had vowed would never happen to me was happening. When I first started in the business, I had told my wife that I would take time to balance work and family life.

Working harder and longer for my family was a lie. I did not realize it, but it was a lie. It was a lie that society has given us. It was too easy to use that as an excuse to work more and spend more time in my work than face the reality that I was spinning inside a hamster wheel. It led me to question many things that were taught to us by our society and falsely spread through mediocrity. From that day onward, I was more aware of how I spent my time. How much time I had spent in my business or on my business compared to how much time with my family. I recruited my wife and daughters to help. I asked them to come to me and pull me away from my work when they wanted a hug or time with me. Imagine what your life would be like if everyone in your family was invested in keeping the family unit happy. Everyone can play an important part in keeping the family together as one cohesive unit. Just remember, you can work hard and play hard but don't ever lose the farm!

Secret # 8

- **Don't be a sheep, be a contrarian.** In my second year in the mortgage brokering business, I was facing the same problems as everyone else. The real estate market was cooling down in a big way and business seemed to be dwindling. What could I do? I looked around and everyone was having the same problem. The government had tightened lending guidelines, which made it more difficult to receive approvals from lenders. This forced many people to give up. Many left the industry or made a switch and became employees with the lenders. I was faced with a dilemma and had tough choices to make. Either go back to the bank as an employee or make another career change. I am glad I did not pick either of those choices. I knew that if I stayed, I had to do something different or achieve similar results as everyone else. I looked around and decided to have faith in myself and go against the grain.

When people stop advertising, I market more and find more avenues to expose myself (not that kind of exposure). When things are going well and my pipeline is full, I go and get more business to push through more. You never know when business is going to slow down. When things are too chaotic, I take time out to meditate or go and reconnect with nature. When people take long holidays off during statutory holidays, I go to work, then go on vacation when they aren't. I prefer to be a big fish in a very small pond than a big whale in the ocean.

Secret # 9

- **Bigger is not better.** I went independent at a time when it seemed that nearly every broker was flocking like sheep to the big brokerage franchises. They said I was crazy and that I wouldn't last long. I did it because I felt and believed it was the right thing to do and not because I wanted to prove them wrong. Like all things, everything has its time and place. Mine was not with a big franchise. They told me that I would lose many lenders and have access to less. I convinced my partner Camilo Rodriguez to leave and take our office independent. We were both scared and thought that the franchise people might be right. I am glad they were wrong. Really, really wrong! Ironically, we gained more brokers that felt the same way we did, and we also received more lender access than when we were with the big franchise. Imagine that! We later found out why.

Not all lenders like to do business with big franchises. Some lenders prefer quality business over quantity. When they work with big franchises, it is much harder for clients to control the quality of each deal since the volume of business makes it difficult to police. Being part of a big franchise has its advantages, but it also has drawbacks. This is one of them. The only thing that a big franchise can offer is their brand and support through their network of brokers. If you are building your own brand, then it may be counterintuitive to partner up with a franchise. The network supports inside a franchise is hit and miss. When I was with them, I was one of a handful that contributed to the "support" in the network by answering questions and requests for assistance from other brokers. Anyone can replicate a support network today through connections on Linkedin or their online "groups." The question is, "Why would a franchise be of benefit to you?" Yes, ask "Why" rather than "How." Do you have to be assimilated into their "collective" and abide by their lists of do's and don'ts, or can you be an independent thinker and still be able to do "your own thing"? Does everything in your business look like an identical clone? Ask any realtor…they'll tell you what I mean.

If you are new to the industry and too scared to start out with an independent brokerage, join one of the franchise offices and learn as fast as you can. Just be aware that opportunity for growth is very limited because a majority of managing brokers do not want to help create more competition for them. There is no incentive for them to help you grow to become a managing broker and build your own team. If you are happy with an average income each year as if you were a bank employee, then you will fit right in with any franchise. I am not a maverick but I don't fit in with the status quo. I am passionate about what I do and love helping other entrepreneurs like myself who want to grow their business so that they can help more people. I love making a difference in people's lives, and the feeling I receive by doing so is immeasurable. It is more rewarding than the monetary gain. Strangely, though, the more people whose lives I help change, the more I gain financially.

Secret # 10

- **Demand your fair share!** You won't get that on commercial financing if you are with the franchise brokerage. They prefer you not do commercial and not train people in it so that the commercial division gets the business and splits with the head office (brokers are only compensated 25% of the money for sending them the lead). I believe a 60/40 percent split would have been more appropriate. Sometimes I even offer 50% if the originating broker contributes to the process. Everything is open to negotiation. I do that with every residential mortgage broker that refers business to me. I recognize that there is value in building the relationship with them and them building a relationship with their client. For those that want the whole pie to themselves, I am willing to train and mentor them.

I teach brokers how to be competent and do well in commercial financing for several reasons. For one, it elevates our profession to a higher level. The more competent we are, the more outstanding the perception of our profession will be by the general public. Letting the residential brokers who want to "try" commercial financing fail will make brokers look bad in the client's eyes. Incompetent brokers will negatively affect the industry. I believe there is so much opportunity out there for everyone even if every broker in the world is capable of doing commercial financing. A broker that is competent at all types of financing has the ability to create multiple streams of income, and that will help them create a good stable future. This in turn will give more credibility to the broker community at large. An industry with a high turnover is not well received by the general public and other professions. If you have a good heart, love this industry and need a mentor, I can help you or find someone who can. You deserve to succeed. This industry could use more people with heart rather than soulless financiers. There are greedy, selfish professionals in our industry, and we can use more good people to offset those people.

Secret # 11

- **What you focus on grows.** Even when others around me have complained about the slowdown in business due to the economy or due to the loss in immigrants, I didn't let it bother me. I feel that there is nothing that I can do to change the economy or bring more immigrants to our country to help boost the real estate market. Why should I waste my time commiserating? Why should I focus on those things that I cannot control or have anything to do with? I have decided long ago to only focus on what I can control – my attitude and my activities. Surprisingly, my business has grown leaps and bounds, year after year. I am grateful and give thanks every night for receiving new clients each and every day. So far, business has been great day after day and year after year. I envision that one day I will have so many referrals that people will come to join our team just to help me take care of those referral clients that keep pouring in. Someone has to help them, why not me? Why not you?

Secret # 12

- **Have an exit strategy… or forever the hamster in the cage.**
  Most of us are working hard at what we do and yet at the end of
  the day, we feel like we have not move far in our lives. Sages have
  said that if you're doing the same thing day after day and expecting
  different results, you're insane. Everyone wants to get ahead in
  life, but only a few dare to chase their dream. That's not you?
  Doesn't apply to you? What is your exit plan? Death is not a good
  exit strategy although it's a sure thing if you want to bet on it.

What is your strategy for receiving passive income so that one day
you won't have to be forced to run on that hamster wheel again?
As much as I love what I do today, I know that I won't be able to
work indefinitely and that one day the energy and excitement may
dwindle. Perhaps I will still be excited, but my physical body may
not want to jump up and down as much anymore. I have an exit
plan: I started working on my business to create residual income.
Believe it or not, I started on my exit plan after my second year in
business. I heard that it's best to plan too early rather than too late.

What is your plan to get out of the "rat race"? Have you started?
Do you know how? Are you working in your business or on your
business? "What's the difference," you ask? There is a big
difference! Can you make money when you are on vacation and
not need to worry about your business imploding? The answer to
that question is the key. I can teach you the difference and show
you exactly how to do it.

Secret # 13

- **I can be No. 1!** I've done it, and so can you. When I first started in the industry and started to market to my target market, I was one of several dozen mortgage brokers. It was a much-targeted niche market, and it was very crowded already. I came with the mentality that I will be number one, not because I was arrogant or knew more than others, but because I just felt that deep down inside, I was the only one with a big heart for my clients and my reason for being in this business was not because of money. I started the business for a cause. Each client I met I told them my story and why I was doing what I was doing. This was not my dream but it was my calling. I know it sounds silly and even a bit strange as I write it today. However, I know that what I do and how I do it can impact people in a big way. I feel that I was one of a few who have integrity and are willing to stand up for the clients -- someone who is thinking about the client's family first rather than the paycheck. I also know that I will always put them before me. I know many preach this gospel but not many actually do it.

Today, I am the number one in my niche market. What did I do? How did I get there? I will share with you the tactics and strategies that have allowed me to reach my current goal. Believe it or not, I am not even half done yet. Imagine what my business will be once I complete my journey and implement the vision that I have.

Secret # 14

- **Don't let one bad seed corrupt the whole harvest!**
Be a world-class professional by always having the right attitude all the time. I check my ego when I get a big deal done. When a deal goes sideways for me, I learn from it and immediately move on. Attitude is everything. One extra minute spent asking what went wrong will create more of the same problems. Focus on how to get it done right next time

When a deal is not going the way that you had planned, let everyone know about it immediately. Clients have expectations but if you keep an open communication with them, they will be the first one to forgive you. They understand that sometimes bad things can happen to good people. My clients amaze me, and they are my heroes. They had the courage to reach out to a stranger to help them with the biggest investment in their life. It is their attitude that keeps me in this business. How often does a stranger come to you for help when their finances are in chaos? They were brave enough to open up to me about their personal financial challenges and aspirations. They put their trust in me long before I even earned it. That to me is amazing. Respect them by having the right attitude even when things don't turn out the way it was planned.

Secret # 15

- **Hire a coach because you don't know Jack!** That is the universal truth: I was naive when I first started in business. I didn't know what I didn't know. I was dangerously enthusiastic about my opportunity and didn't know any better. It was like a shaken soda bottle about to be uncapped. I wanted to be successful and was willing to do whatever it took. I thought I had the right attitude. Those people who said "attitude was everything" must have left out a few things. After several miserable failures and loss of money, I admitted I was not where I wanted to be. I didn't realize I was not prepared to achieve success. I didn't know that you must grow personally to achieve success. It seems that this is a universal truth that is often ignored or not given enough attention. The truth is that most people including myself are not ready for success. Mentally, I was not prepared. I didn't realize it at that time and needed a few humble pies dished out at me. I know that my work is only half done and that I will encounter many more humbling moments in the future.

I quickly learned that all the great and successful people in sports or business all had one thing in common. They had a coach to help them. The coach would help lift up the "blinders" that I often have on so that I can see more clearly. I can stay more focused and work smarter. I will still encounter situations that I may fail at but at least I will be more aware of it and welcome the opportunity.

The more I learn from my failures, the more I will grow and be more prepared. The more I grow, the better I will become, and that will allow me to reach plateaus that I have only dreamed about. After investing tens of thousands of dollars on business coaches and mentors, I can unequivocally attest that this is what made the most impact on my success so far.

One word of caution, your first coach may not be the right fit for you. Randomly picking any business coach or mentor out there will only guarantee a tax write-off and not results. Find out what you are weak at and search for the coach that is strong in that area to help you grow. One coach may not be sufficient but hiring too many may be a waste of your money. I have two or three at any given time. I enlist in more when I require assistance in a particular area. This is not a rule of thumb. Only you know how much help you need.

Conclusion

My vision is to directly train and mentor 50 individuals to become superstars and they can help replicate the process to help thousands more. People in the industry feel that we are saturated with brokers. I don't believe that to be true. Brokers in countries such as Europe, Australia and USA have more than 60-70% market shares and they have more than ten times the amount of brokers. I would like to help change that. Another thing that I am working on changing is the perception that independent brokers have against bank employees. They view bankers as competitors. I do not view the bankers and bank representatives as competitors but rather colleagues doing our best with our own toolset that we have. I have come to call many of these so called competitors as friends over the years.

It may come as a surprise to many bank executives but many bank managers and their advisors have referred me business that they could not help at their bank. They do it even at the risk of losing their job. They are the unsung heroes for having the courage to refer the business out so that they could help the client instead of letting the client hang to dry. Not every client will fit a lender's guideline. As a former bank employee myself, I understand what it is like being an employee of the bank and not able to help everyone out. It feels bad and nobody wants to be the bad guy. Everyone wants to be a hero. When we treat each other as allies, then together we can accomplish the goal of helping virtually every client. If you would like to join me and embrace this movement, I guarantee you that you will get referrals from the bank rather than only referring clients to the bank. I will also guarantee that you will have allies instead of enemies. Bankers can and will become your ambassadors.

If you don't believe that is possible for you, I challenge you to come to my workshop. What do you have to lose? What can you gain?

Gratitude & Thank you

I grew up in a successful entrepreneurial family and just like my father; I had acquired the entrepreneurial spirit at a young age. I knew what hard work was and worked hard at whatever business I was involved in. I have had successful business ventures in the commercial fishing industry, construction trades, restaurant business and the financial services industry today.

Helping people has always been the biggest motivating factor for me. You can say I am intrinsically motivated. I love to help people and make a difference in their life.

In less than 4 years as a mortgage broker, I have become the #1 mortgage broker in the Vietnamese community! I have grown my business by nearly fourfold at a time when many people were leaving or consider leaving the industry. I am grateful that I have done so well when most of my colleagues have experienced a downturn in the industry. I am eternally grateful for my clients, friends and family whom have supported me all these years. Without them I would not be where I am today.

I believe a big part of my success has been how I do business and my clients can see that I have similar values as them. I share them my story and genuinely treat my clients as if they were a member of my family. I have always aimed to go above and beyond my "job title". My clients know why I do what I do. Knowing what I stand for has allowed me to attract the best clients anyone would be envious of!

By being selective with whom I work with, I am able to work around my family time and truly dedicate my life to the most important people in my life. Many of my clients have become great friends and even consider them as family.

I truly believe that you can have everything in life that you want, just as long as you help enough people get what they want first! I wholeheartedly embrace the teachings of Zig Ziglar. Thanks Zig!

Thank you for reading my story and I look forward to hearing from you.

Gift to you

FREE Exclusive Bonus $397 Value: In gratitude for purchasing my book, I would like to offer you a gift to attend my interactive workshop. I normally charge $397 for this workshop, but for you it is **absolutely free!**

This 3 hours long intensive workshop which will cover the following advanced training:
- ✓ Effective niche marketing - how you can lower your costs, simplify your marketing, and still become the biggest fish in your small pond.
- ✓ Effective sales funnel – how to create loyal, "value oriented" clients instead of competing in the race to the bottom (price oriented clients).
- ✓ Contrarian lead generation strategies – how to generate leads from the least likely sources.
- ✓ Orchestrating your brand & how to win sponsors – how to become the "go to expert" in your particular niche and have people raving about you!
- ✓ Build promotional and production partners – how to create multiple sources of active leads through synergistic partnerships.

To receive this offer, email your contact information to info@SuaTruong.com with subject line: Contrarian Marketing Workshop.

2nd Bonus Gift:

Go to www.SharingBankSecrets.com to learn many financial insider bank secrets and tips that are not commonly known. Also keep abreast of recent news and changes in the industry that you can take advantage of.

Learn how to get free service and products from your banks and many other ways to save you thousands of dollars over the years.

<u>Additional benefits for signing up:</u>
• **E-book :** future e-books will be offered to help you get ahead financially.
• **Exclusive Invitations**: Get invitations to special limited-time workshops on finances and practical real estate investment strategies.

3rd Bonus Gift: Goal <u>Achieving</u> Book. Getting goals and achieving them are a vital part of success. But this is not a goal-setting book, so I can't go into more detail on how to set or achieve goals. However, my mentor and friend Raymond Aaron, recognized as the world's #1 authority on goal achievement, has written a bestselling hardcover book *Double Your Income Doing What You Love.* On the back cover, there are testimonials from giant celebrities who use his program. One such testimonial is by Jack Canfield, the co-creator of the *Chicken Soup for the Soul* series of books. Here is his testimonial: "The reason I personally chose to use this amazing system for myself and for my company is that, bluntly stated, it is the most power system ever created." By special arrangement, I have permission to allow you, my dear reader, to own a copy of Mr. Aaron's book for free and you can get it by instant download simply by going to his website, www.aaron.com.

Made in the USA
Charleston, SC
06 February 2015